7 Paths to Managerial Leadership

7 Paths to Managerial Leadership

Leadership

Fred Mackenzie

Library of Congress Control Number:		2012910172
ISBN:	Hardcover	978-1-4771-2480-2
	Softcover	978-1-4771-2479-6
	Ebook	978-1-4771-2481-9

To order additional copies of this book, contact:
Xlibris Corporation
1-888-795-4274
www.Xlibris.com
Orders@Xlibris.com
111157

Contents

To Nancy R. Lee

Enlightened scholar and steadfast supporter
without whom this book would never have been written

Managers and Subordinates

A Dynamic Relationship

This book is for you, the manager and supervisor of others.

There are many good books on management ranging all the way from strategic planning to decision-making. Also, there has been a steady stream of insightful books on leadership, describing those attributes necessary for inspiring others to have confidence in *you, the leader.*

This book is about Managerial Leadership, the art of getting exceptional work done through the willing efforts of your subordinates. It focuses on action, not position. It inspires subordinates to have confidence in *themselves.*

The 7 Paths approach in this book is a middle management presentation of the work of Nancy R. Lee (*The Practice of Managerial Leadership*, Xlibris, 2007) and Elliott Jaques (*Requisite Organization*, Cason Hall, 2006).

You may remember your first role as a manager of others, as someone who gets work done through the efforts of other people. You were probably promoted because of your excellence as an individual contributor—you got *your* work done! And perhaps upper management thought you had an above-average "feel" for working with others. However, managing others is more than getting along; it involves deciding who can do the work, who needs coaching on specific assignments, who can be left alone to get a task accomplished, and who needs development in their role. All managers carry this managerial leadership accountability.

To quote Jaques, "*Managerial teamworking* is the most powerful leadership-enhancing mechanism of all. In effective teamworking, the strength of the mutual influencing between a manager and a subordinate reaches its highest level, context setting, and mutual understanding are at their clearest. There is an immediate sharing of values, and there results the greatest possibility of maximum commitment by all to the achievement of commonly valued goals."

Managerial Leadership combines the discipline of managing a unit with the skill of allowing subordinates to work at their level of capability, grow in their role, and produce extraordinary results. It focuses on managers reaching their full potential and, at the same time, inspiring members of their team to do the same. This, in turn, increases the effectiveness of the total organization.

Figure 1

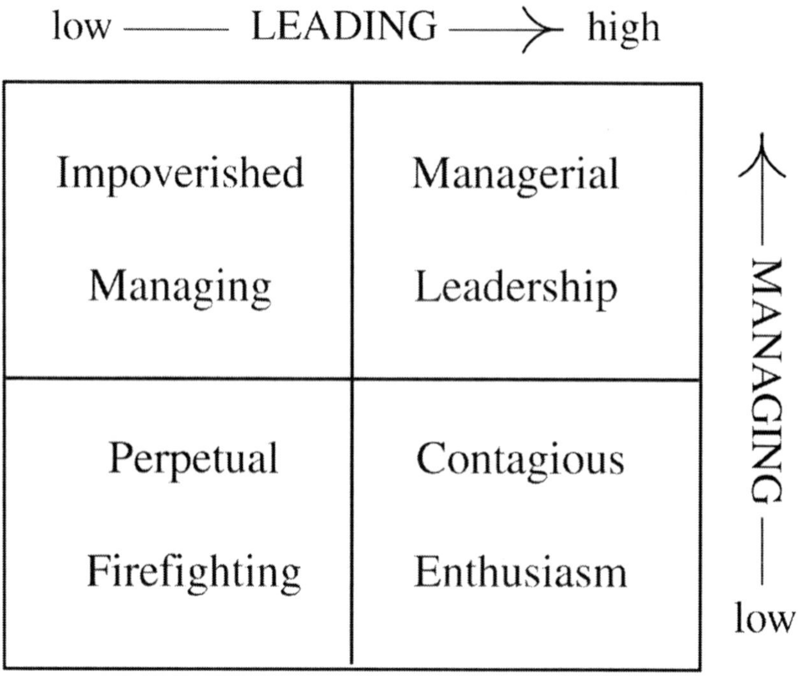

low ——— LEADING ——⟶ high

Impoverished Managing	Managerial Leadership
Perpetual Firefighting	Contagious Enthusiasm

MANAGING

high ←——— MANAGING ——— low

Figure 1 reflects the results of hundreds of observations of the styles of middle managers:

The upper left window (Impoverished Managing) describes managers who are high on managerial skills but lack the people orientation to allow subordinates to be self-motivated. They tend to micromanage their subordinates and seek perfection. Feedback is generally negative, and there is little managerial coaching.

The lower right window (Contagious Enthusiasm) includes those who are optimistic, inspirational, and wonderful to be around. Their interpersonal skills are great, and people follow their direction. However, their managerial skills of planning, organizing, implementing, and evaluating are lacking. This often happens when a person is promoted from being successful as an individual contributor to a managerial position without the necessary management training.

The lower left window (Perpetual Firefighting) represents those individuals who have little or no skills in either leadership or management. These people exist as managers, but usually not for long. Their workday involves putting out fires, planning for contingencies, and trying to survive. They work hard but make little progress.

The upper right window (Managerial Leadership) includes managers who combine their managerial skills with the understanding and practice of involving their subordinates in the goals of the unit. Their vocabulary includes such words as participation, empowerment, enabling, growth, context setting, and collaboration. As a unit, they meet or exceed their goals.

All managers are somewhere along the LEADING scale and somewhere along the MANAGING scale. Which is your primary window, the one from which you see the world of work?

When we examine the key elements of highly successful organizations, an effective manager–subordinate relationship stands out as one of the foundational links in getting the work done. Strategies, long-range plans, corporate objectives are all important, but the cascading of accountabilities and task assignments to the operational level is what results in work output. This relationship must be clear, honest, trusting, and continuous. It is a major part of every manager's job. To quote Nancy Lee, "The most important relationship in a managerial hierarchy is that of a manager and a subordinate. Managers are persons in a role in which they are held accountable not only for doing their best personally but also for the results of the work and the results of the working behavior of their subordinates."

Have you ever had a boss like this?

"Welcome to the unit. I am your manager, and I will be laying out the work I expect you to do. Don't argue with me. If you have a question, ask someone in the unit. Don't bring me problems. I expect you to solve them yourself. If you do well, we'll get along. If you don't get done what I expect, I'll get someone else to replace you. Do I make myself clear?"

Or this?

"Welcome to the unit. I am your manager, and I have written out a list of things you and I will be working on. Read it over and put down any questions you may have. Let's get together tomorrow morning at 9:00 to finalize the list and put some completion dates down. Now, I'd like to take you around to meet your colleagues who will help you get oriented. It's good to have you on board."

Exit interview studies have indicated that most people do not leave an organization because they dislike the organization; they leave because they do not like their boss and the way they are supervised. In a recent survey of eleven thousand employees, 36 percent said they do not know what their manager wants from them. Both of these examples reflect a serious breakdown in the critical manager–subordinate relationship. This book is based on 7 approaches to the development of an effective relationship between the manager and his or her subordinates.

Guidelines for an effective manager–subordinate relationship

- ❖ Keep discussions on an adult to adult basis, not parent to child.
- ❖ The goal is mutual trust achieved through openness and clarity.
- ❖ Exercise managerial leadership, not managerial dictatorship.
- ❖ Encourage feedback from subordinates.
- ❖ Remember, this is a two-way working relationship.
- ❖ The relationship is continuous and dynamic.

The 7 Paths to Managerial Leadership described in this book are as follows:

1. Managerial Planning and Task Assignment
2. Managerial Meetings
3. Context Setting
4. Feedback
5. Performance Appraisal
6. Coaching Subordinates
7. Continual Improvement

These 7 Paths contain practices that are based on sound, proven principles covering decades of evaluation and fine-tuning. Simply stated, they determine

- the tasks that need to be accomplished.
- the focus on continuous feedback to subordinates.
- the evaluation of the work obtained.

My experience in applying these principles as a manager has shown that subordinates like the way these practices work and become more productive. This positive attitude and behavior lead to a motivated and productive work unit.

I suggest you review the 7 Paths, select the ones that go with the grain of your thinking, and start doing those. Once these are underway, go back and look at the remaining ones and select one or more to experiment with. In time, you may find that all the practices will help you develop a high-performing team you will be proud of. Becoming a competent managerial leader will result in less firefighting, less overtime work, and an overall reduction of your stress level.

The paths are sequenced in the order they usually occur. The first, Managerial Planning and Task Assignment, is probably the most detailed to apply, but this path is the core of any management system. This is an excellent place to start. Spending some time improving where you are as "a manager of others" instead of pondering where you should be will be the key to your continued success.

Leo Tolstoy, the great Russian novelist, once said, *"Everyone thinks of changing the world, but no one thinks of changing himself."* This book will help you change yourself as a manager. Read it with a pencil handy.

Why the 7 Paths?

The Human Forces Filter

The 7 Paths is an effective way to combat an unconscious false assumption that managers have been making for decades: that, given clear assignments, employees will produce precisely what the manager expects.

Every organization starts with an idea, a purpose, and a plan. Based on this plan, an organization structure is put together. This structure is composed of roles or positions showing what roles report directly to the CEO or President and what roles report to these senior positions and so on. Staffing follows, placing people in the roles who are judged capable of doing the work of the role.

It is assumed that if the assignments in a role are clear and there is an individual who has the necessary qualifications to fill the role, then that person will complete the work as specified and the organization will receive the results expected.

In real life, this assumption turns out not to be always true. Over and over again, we hear managers saying, *"We are not getting the results we should be getting given the people and resources we have."*

Figure 2 illustrates the assumed sequence to work output.

Figure 2

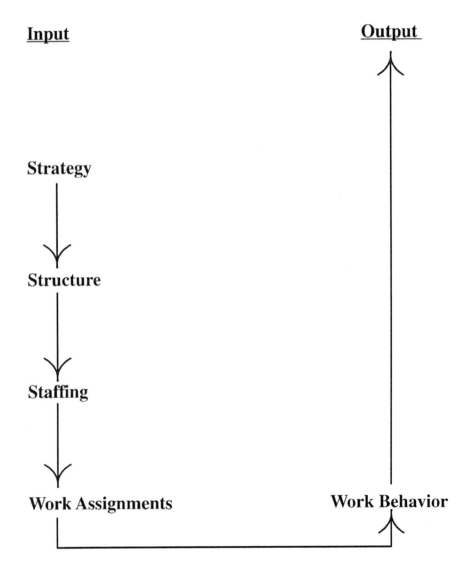

Input

Output

Strategy

Structure

Staffing

Work Assignments

Work Behavior

Figure 3

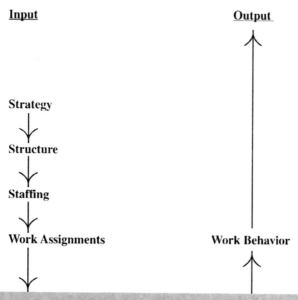

Input   **Output**

Strategy

Structure

Staffing

Work Assignments   Work Behavior

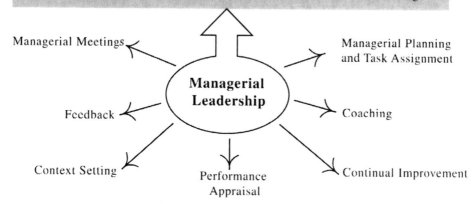

Influences on Individual Behavior
Personal Values — Organization Culture — Skills Knowledge — Habits
Unclear Communications — Motivation — Personal Goals — Self Image

Managerial Meetings   Managerial Planning
                                       and Task Assignment

**Managerial
Leadership**

Feedback   Coaching

Context Setting   Continual Improvement

Performance
Appraisal

Figure 3 shows the fundamental reason why this sequence does not automatically happen and how the 7 Paths can significantly improve the desired results.

A person's behavior toward a given goal goes through a filter that influences the work output. It is called the Human Forces Filter. This filter is different for each employee and includes such things as:

- The work values the person has developed over years
- The organization culture
- The person's relationship with his or her manager
- The skills and knowledge the individual has (or does not have)
- The habits acquired over time
- The person's own goals at any given time
- What is understood or not understood about their assignments
- What actually motivates the individual
- The person's self-image

An employee's work behavior is distorted by his or her unique prism and often results in a somewhat different output from what was expected by the manager. The 7 Paths to Managerial Leadership is an excellent way to minimize these individual differences. Meaningful new approaches, processes, and procedures are presented, which, when implemented and become habits, will result in improved work behavior for both the managers and their subordinates. Following these paths will:

- ✓ replace bad habits with good habits
- ✓ build teamwork
- ✓ involve subordinates in unit thinking
- ✓ clarify task assignments that must be done
- ✓ allow for mature (adult to adult) dialogue
- ✓ foster individual growth
- ✓ facilitate improvement through proper coaching
- ✓ ensure ongoing performance effectiveness
- ✓ utilize both positive and constructive feedback

It is not the intention of using the 7 Paths to change an employee's personality, individual values, or personal goals. The objective is to enable improvement and growth of the subordinate, help build the team, maintain a stimulating environment, and produce outstanding results. That is Managerial Leadership.

This approach is not an overnight solution. It is a journey that develops Managerial Leadership. It is a guide for managers to improve their practices in three areas:

- *Defining* the individual tasks that need to be accomplished
- *Providing* ongoing feedback to subordinates
- *Evaluating* the results of task completion

Start with one path, then another. You will find the process a powerful and refreshing experience for you and your subordinates.

Path 1

MANAGERIAL PLANNING AND TASK ASSIGNMENT

Establishing Accountabilities

Managerial Planning

Managers plan what has to be done in their unit, by whom, by when, and how best to use available resources. To do this requires a clear vision of what is required to be done, how to carry out the manager's role, and the skill in communicating it to the team.

Managers complete a task in three ways:

- They do it themselves.
- They complete it with the help of a subordinate.
- They delegate it to a subordinate.

When defining tasks for a subordinate, there are four things for a manager to specify: Quantity, Quality, completion Time, and available Resources (QQTR). A task can be defined as a *"what by when."*

Managers should encourage subordinates to participate in the task assignment process by providing input, detailing possible action steps, and examining various approaches to task completion. However, the manager makes the final work planning decisions. When delegating a task, the manager should enable the subordinate to report back when conditions have changed, and there is a possibility of the assignment not being completed to QQTR.

This is a good time to rate yourself as to how well you are presently planning the work in your unit. Put an X anywhere along the scale where you believe best describes your present performance.

Self Assessment

Managerial Planning

0	1	2	3	4	5

I do little detailed
planning of the work
in my unit

I do some
overall planning
annually

I plan the work
of each subordinate
on an ongoing basis

Have you ever experienced a situation like the following?

"Hey Joe, how are you coming along on the procedure manual for the new copy machine assembly line?"

"I've given it to Mary to do, John, but she has been very busy with her regular work. I'll check into it, and let you know."

"Well, you recall I mentioned it to you a couple of weeks ago. My boss says he wants to show it to the VPs next month at the big meeting."

"I don't think we can get it done that fast, John, with vacations and all. Helen has been out on maternity leave, and I'm not sure when she's coming back. As you know, Mary is doing some of Helen's work."

"Joe, I don't want excuses—this is high priority for my boss, and I'm in trouble if we don't produce. And you know what that means!"

The first step in Managerial Planning is to be clear on what is expected from your managerial role. Specifically,

- what you are accountable for?
- what unit, functional or departmental goals, are assigned to you?
- what resources (people, funds, etc.) do you have?

Without clarity here, anything you do can be misdirected and, unfortunately in the end, unappreciated. Your manager may not be used to giving you clear, specific goals with appropriate resources, but this information is essential to your ongoing success. From my experience, at the beginning of a work cycle, one or more frank discussions with your boss clarifying your accountabilities are a must. Good managers have clear purpose.

There's an old German proverb that says: "*What's the use of running if you are not on the right path*" and, in this instance, the right 7 Paths to Managerial Leadership.

As a manager, you have the accountability to get certain things accomplished beyond what you can physically do yourself. That's why you have subordinates to help you. It's your job to set out "who is going to do what." In other words, this work planning process consists of determining what has to be done and which subordinate is able to complete which assignment.

The process of Managerial Planning also includes the accountability for building an effective ongoing team taking into consideration

- who needs specific coaching if they are to complete a new task?
- who needs development in their current role?
- who is ready and willing to take on more responsibility?

Managerial Planning—A Summary

- ✓ Managers plan how to accomplish the work of their unit.
- ✓ Managers should not delegate this planning to subordinates.

✓ Subordinates can help in detailing the manager's plan.
✓ Managers should discuss work planning options with subordinates whenever possible and seek their suggestions.
✓ Managers make the work planning decisions for their unit.

Action Planning

Review the self-assessment you did earlier on your managerial planning. List some possible action plans you would like to implement over the next six months regarding your managerial planning. Here are some examples:

- Generate a list of tasks that you are presently doing that could possibly be delegated (or partially delegated) to one or more subordinates, with the list to be completed by the end of this month (date).
- By (date), conduct a meeting with all subordinates for the purpose of getting feedback as to how well your planning of the unit's work is functioning, including suggestions as to how it might be improved.
- By (date), review the completion dates of all subordinates' task assignments and prepare a schedule of informal discussions with each subordinate as to the progress being made.

_____
_____
_____
_____
_____
_____

Task Assignment

There are two types of assignments contained in any role. The first are the *Specific Tasks* assigned to the role. The second are *General Responsibilities* assigned to the role.

Some organizations combine the two under the heading "Role Accountabilities." By listing the high priority items (perhaps 4 to

6 for each type), focus can then be directed to what is called "Key Accountabilities," those that comprise the most important work to be done and hence the most important factors for the performance appraisal. "Key Accountabilities," the key specific Task Assignments plus the key General Responsibilities, typically account for about 80 percent of the effort of the individual in the role.

When a subordinate's accomplishments are lagging behind expectations, many times it is because of lack of clarity. Clear task assignments are the core of any management system. They are central to building trust within the organization.

As you did for Managerial Planning, rate yourself as to how well you are assigning tasks in your unit.

Self Assessment

Task Assignment

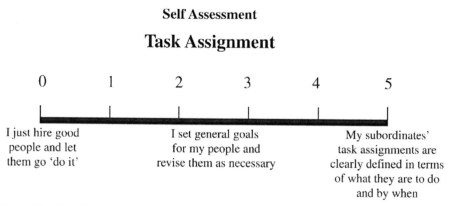

Specific Tasks

The person who starts out going nowhere in particular, generally gets there.

A specific task is an assignment` to produce a desired result within a time frame where quality, quantity, and resources are prescribed. It has three parts: the verb that denotes closure, the subject, and the completion or milestone date.

Here are some examples:

Complete   proposal for revised vacation plan   by 7/31/xx

Submit	recommendations for an onboarding program	by 8/31/xx
Reduce	avoidable turnover by 10% compared to the average for the years 20xx-20yy	by 12/31/xx
Increase	by 15% customer satisfaction ratings over 20yy	by 1/2/xx
Achieve	profit of minimum $200K from P and S Projects	by 12/31/xx
Provide	up-to-date budget information to chief accountant for use in budget consolidation	at end of each month beginning 1/31/xx
Conduct	three customer relations workshops for new salespeople	by 7/1/20xx
Establish	a security procedure for after-hours entry into building	by 4/30/20xx
Generate	a draft policy for relocation expenses	by 9/1/20xx
Identify	four possible store locations in Ohio	by 1/1/20xx

When writing a specific task assignment, the sentence should start with a verb that describes closure, not just an activity. When using activity verbs (e.g. understand, ensure, assist, investigate, support, help, champion) task results are difficult to measure and to determine completion times. Therefore, they are not suitable for writing task assignments.

Following are some sample closure verbs:

Key Closure Verbs	Also Usable	Usable with added Closure Verb
Achieve	Appraise	Advise and . . .
Audit	Approve	Analyze and . . .
Close	Assign	Apply and . . .
Complete	Attend	Arrange and . . .
Conduct	Authorize	Assure and . . .
Consolidate	Classify	Check and . . .
Eliminate	Construct	Consolidate and . . .
Establish	Create	Describe and . . .
Evaluate	Design	Determine and
Generate	Deliver	Develop and . . .
Identify	Distribute	Inspect and . . .
Implement	Execute	Interview and . . .
Initiate	Issue	Perform and . .
Manage	Open	Prepare and . . .
Obtain	Provide	Review and . . .
Recommend	Select	Revise and . . .
Schedule	Summarize	Transmit and . .
Sell	Test	Update and . . .
Submit	Train	Verify and . . .

As mentioned earlier, each assigned task has a Quantity, Quality, completion Time, and allocated Resources aspect to it. This is called the QQTR. Usually, the quantity and time are easy to specify where describing the quality and resources desired are not. Many times quality is covered through company policy and normal expectations (e.g. a selection procedure meeting company affirmative action policy, a safety rule conforming to OSHA requirements). Resources can be more difficult and are usually understood between the manager and the subordinate. However, when necessary, they can be specific in terms of available funds, manpower, access to information, and so on. What is important is to have the desired quality and available resources clearly understood.

As will happen from time to time, circumstances will change and a specific task will need to be revised to fit the new situation. In instances where circumstances make it likely that outputs cannot be achieved as specified, or that more could be done, subordinates are accountable to inform the manager in time for adaptive action to be taken. In this way, there will be no surprises. Here, the subordinate may be able to suggest possible options for the revised task. However, the manager decides what is to be done, including whatever changes are needed in the task assignment.

General Responsibilities

The other type of task assignment are those that fall under the heading "General Responsibilities." These assignments are ongoing in nature. Examples are as follows:

1. Maintain ongoing monthly contact with key customers.
2. Keep abreast of changes in Italian legislation on imports into Italy.
3. Keep informed about the marketing strategy of the top two competitors regarding their new products.

Sometimes specific tasks occur as a part of a general responsibility. Using the three examples of general responsibilities above, specific tasks might be as follows:

1. Conduct a two-day annual key customer convention in Chicago in August, 20xx with a budget not to exceed $yyyy.
2. Obtain translated copies of the new Italian import legislation and present a summary at the marketing meeting in September, 20xx.
3. Submit a report and present findings on new product launching strategy by our two major competitors at marketing meeting in May, 20xx."

For a more detailed explanation of task assignments, key accountabilities, and general responsibilities, see Appendix A titled *"Establishing Key Accountabilities."*

Another aspect of writing task assignments is making sure that individual assignments align with the goals of the manager and the manager's manager and so on up the ladder to the overall goals of the organization. Appendix B, *"Making Strategy Work—The Linkage Process"* sets out the entire system of aligning individual's accountabilities and task assignments with the overall strategy of the organization. Step four in Appendix B is this final linkage and is especially worth reading.

Linking long-range strategy to individual key accountabilities transforms broad strategic plans into focused operational plans where all employees understand and feel part of the overall direction and thrust of the organization, both in the short-term and the long-term.

Getting Unit Work Done Effectively—A Summary

Successful managers

- ✓ are clear about their own work.
- ✓ establish subordinates' task assignments.
- ✓ ensure that these tasks are within subordinates' capability.
- ✓ discuss tasks with subordinates before finalizing.
- ✓ assign tasks specifying parameters (QQTR).
- ✓ establish task reporting procedures.
- ✓ review with subordinates their key general responsibilities.

Action Planning

Now that you have some guidelines as to how best to assign tasks to your subordinates, it is time to consider some action planning. Review the self-assessment you did earlier on Task Assignment. Research indicates that "reality" from subordinates' assessments on your managerial leadership practices is about 23 percent lower on average than your self-rating.

Using your newfound skill of writing clear task assignments, prepare some actions on Task Assignment that you would like to accomplish within the next three months.

Here are some examples:

- Schedule a meeting in early January 20xx with all direct reports to explain the QQTR approach to task assignments.
- By February 1, 20xx, implement the QQTR format in all task assignment descriptions.
- Schedule a meeting with each subordinate to discuss progress on task assignments and what barriers may be in the way of getting the task done to QQTR. Discuss any possible changes required and options. Meetings to be completed by April 1, 20xx.
- By May 1, 20xx, revise subordinates' previously written task assignments being sure to include closure verbs and specific completion times.
- Review with each subordinate their 4 to 6 key general responsibilities and what specific tasks may develop from them in the next six months.

_____

_____

_____

_____

_____

_____

Put on your calendar the preparation dates for your action planning. You have now completed the first critical element of Managerial Leadership.

Situational Courage

Before we move on to Path 2, it is worth mentioning something I call *Situational Courage*. This is a two-way process (subordinate-to-manager and manager-to-subordinate). It is not a one-way street.

Subordinates need to have the *courage* to speak up and explain a problem situation from their point of view. This could be such things as changing timelines, requesting additional resources, or discussing changes in anticipated results. It can occur when getting an assignment, changes in the assignment, getting feedback during an assignment, or receiving a performance appraisal. It can also be due to the need to report changes in external circumstances.

Managers need to have the *courage* to invite this discussion and allow it to really happen. They should listen actively and incorporate any thoughts that could improve the situation. Many managers believe they have an "open-door" policy. Sometimes, it is perceived by the subordinate as a "burned bridge" policy.

Managers don't always have all the right answers and many times input from subordinates improve the results. Of course, the manager has the final decision, but a courageous discussion at the right time is usually beneficial to all.

Path 2

MANAGERIAL MEETINGS

Effective and Purposeful

Managers need to have regular meetings with their subordinates for the purpose of problem solving, discussing ideas for solutions, reviewing priorities, setting context, and other situations requiring two-way communications. There are different types of meetings ranging from idea generation to information sharing. Group meetings reduce the tendency for the creation of "silos" between functions that are subordinate to a single manager, encouraging and enabling cross-functional work flow.

As you did in Path 1, rate yourself as to how well you are now conducting your managerial meetings with your team.

Self Assessment

Managerial Meetings

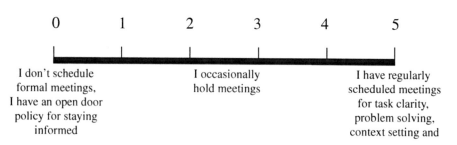

| 0 | 1 | 2 | 3 | 4 | 5 |

I don't schedule
formal meetings,
I have an open door
policy for staying
informed

I occasionally
hold meetings

I have regularly
scheduled meetings
for task clarity,
problem solving,
context setting and

"That was a pretty good meeting we just had with the boss. It solved one of my problems I've been having with Sales."

"Well, it didn't help me. I wanted to get the team's opinion on an idea I had, but there was no time. Now I'll have to go it alone. By the way, I saw Mike Robbins, the software vender coming out of your office yesterday."

"Yeah, we are looking into a program Mike has that would help us handshake our weekly results into the new SAP system."

"Wow! Mike did something like that for us before you joined the team. It cost over thirty thousand dollars and never worked right. Before you go any further with Robbins, I'd be happy to meet with you and walk through the problems we had and perhaps save you some time and budget."

"That would be great. I had a feeling something wasn't quite right."

The above is a typical conversation where one team member was not aligned with the meeting agenda. This occurs when the manager does not communicate the purpose of the meeting ahead of time, does not distribute an agenda outlining the main focus points, and does not ask for suggestions of items to be included. When this is the case, the meeting becomes a free-for-all with everyone trying to get their "oar in the water." This type of meeting usually runs overtime and is not very effective.

With regular context setting meetings, the situation described would not have occurred as everyone would have known about the past problems with Mike's vendor company and alerted the newcomer to the potential pitfalls.

The Process and Content of Meetings

There are two parts to any meeting: the *content* (the what) and the *process* (the how). Let's start with the content of managerial meetings and the subjects that could be covered.

The Content of Managerial Meetings

1. *Unit work review meetings*

In past years, the most common meeting was the Monday morning operations meeting—a review of the present status and what needs to get done this week. This was prevalent in such industries as manufacturing and retail.

The concept of reviewing unit work as a team still exists, but the frequency and type of the meetings have often changed. Now the focus is on task assignment progress, clarifying peer and cross-functional issues, and revising time lines. Depending upon the type of work, these kinds of meetings can be scheduled as much as a month apart and can even be held via teleconferencing when distances are significant.

2. *Idea generation and problem-solving meetings*

On occasion, there can be a need to have your team (or part of your team) join you to help explore possible solutions to a major problem or plan an approach to an upcoming project or issue. This is especially important if they will be part of the execution of the solution.

Participation leads to Involvement.

Involvement leads to Commitment.

Commitment leads to Motivation.

Brainstorming techniques work well in coming up with new ideas and approaches to a difficult issue. It is important to note that in this type of meeting, the manager is seeking information from the subordinates that allows him/her to make a good decision. Consensus is not the goal here.

3. *Communication meetings*

From time to time, a major event occurs that needs to be communicated down the line. It may be a downsizing of the organization, a closing of a product line, a reduction in the overall budget expenditure, a significant change in the structure and people at the top, a takeover by another organization, or some other situation that could be negatively perceived.

Before false rumors start emerging, it is best that meetings occur throughout the organization to communicate the facts and answer questions as accurately as possible at the time. A written communiqué from the top can also be issued to all concerned on the subject, but that by itself does not allow for the personal interaction between the boss and subordinates where the trust relationship helps maintain the morale and motivation of employees during periods of organizational crisis. Countless incidents of this nature have been mishandled, resulting in work-time loss, destructive rumors, and, in some instances, loss of valuable talent.

4. *Individual meetings*

Not all meetings need to be group oriented. The manager will often want and need to discuss a task assignment with a subordinate. This can occur when a new task is being assigned or the QQTR of an existing task is not on track (e.g., the completion time is running into difficulty) or there is a change in the outcome desired.

The Process of Managerial Meetings

Now let's look at the *process* of meetings. It is here where much energy, time, and resources can be saved when certain principles are implemented.

"Hey Joe, I'd like to get together with you to discuss our unit's role in this cross-functional project on the new acquisition. When's a good time?"

"Helen, I'd love to work with you on this, but I am tied up in meetings all week, and Sunday I leave for a plant visit in Mexico. As you know, I am on six different committees. They are all meeting for the quarterly reports when I return which means I don't have any free time until next month. I'm sorry."

"I understand, but this is important to the smooth integration of our function with the acquisition. Next month will be too late. I guess I'll just go it alone. I'll send you copies of my recommendations. Have a good trip."

The above dialog actually happened with one of my clients. Meetings had become such a dominate way of life in this organization that no time was available to sit down with another person to discuss an imminent critical issue.

A mature team, with good meeting skills, should be able to conclude a productive meeting in one hour or less. What needs to be done to hold an effective meeting? The following list describes some proven techniques used in successful managerial meetings. You can add your own to the list:

- Not all subordinates need to be at all meetings. Be selective and let non-attendees get on with their work. Put them on the list to receive a summary of the meeting so they don't think they are missing out.
- Send out a brief agenda so that people can get organized and bring the proper data to the meeting. State what kind of meeting it will be (work status, context setting, problem solving, etc.). Include the starting and finishing times in the agenda.

- Stick to the time frame. Start on time whether or not everyone has arrived. They will soon learn you mean what you say regarding the start time. Besides, it is wasteful for the rest of the team to wait for one or two stragglers, and it extends the overall time of the meeting.
- Finish on time even though everything hasn't been accomplished. Everyone will quickly adjust to this and work toward completion in subsequent meetings.

  The following actually happened in a large company headquartered in New York City. A top-level meeting had been going on without any sign of closure. It was 5:00 pm, and one of the vice presidents got up and started to leave the room:

  President: *Where are you going, Bill—we're not finished yet?*

  Vice president: *John, we've been at this for three hours with no conclusions. I've got a train to catch so I'll be home with my family by dinnertime. There is nothing more I can add at this time.*

  This actually broke up the meeting. The president was quite disturbed at the time but admitted later that he learned something.

- Designate someone in the room as the timekeeper, letting the team know that "we are thirty minutes into the meeting and only covered the first item on the agenda," or "there are only ten minutes left and we should begin to summarize our conclusions."
- Have a computer projector, flip chart, or white board in the room so that everyone sees the same data (options, conclusions, next steps, etc.). Without this, people leave with their own notes which are certain not to be the same. The manager can designate someone in the room to be the scribe.
- If possible, have a clock on the wall for all to see.
- Start a meeting at 11:00 a.m. or 4:00 p.m. It's amazing how quickly things get done.
- Discourage (or even eliminate) the use of personal electronics during the meeting.
- Before deciding to have a meeting, think whether a teleconference could accomplish the same thing. Sometimes, a short teleconference prior to a meeting can save time at the

meeting (data to bring, who will make a brief presentation on what, meeting results expected, etc.).

- If at all possible, a summary by the manager of the meeting should go out to all team members indicating what was accomplished, what was not accomplished, and action agreed upon, including the date, time, and location of a follow-up meeting if one is necessary. This step may appear redundant, but it is also a learning device and future team meetings will benefit from "closing the loop."
- About halfway through the meeting, "suspend business" for two minutes and declare a "time out" to discuss how the process is working. Are we on track or off on a tangent? Is everyone participating as expected? Will we finish on time? Should we save one topic for another time? This brief interlude helps to focus the group back on the purpose of the meeting and the agenda.
- There are times when it is worthwhile to combine two types of meetings within one session for efficiency. This works well providing the two are clearly identified and separated. For example, it may be beneficial to have a problem solving meeting followed by a context setting meeting (or vice versa) all within two hours. A break between the two helps to change the mind-set.
- Keep members aware of the cost of meetings. I once had a small machine I bought in Finland that, by imputing the salaries of the people at the meeting, it would operate like a taxi meter giving you the ongoing cost of the meeting. When people saw the thousands of dollars accumulating, it made a definite impact on the length of the meeting. Today, this can easily be done with a bit of software and projected on a screen. Meetings cost money. Long meetings waste money.

Reducing thirty minutes per meeting throughout the organization yields a great deal of manpower savings over the course of a year. It is impressive to do the calculations. Lord Chesterfield said, "Take care of the minutes, and the hours will take care of themselves." But it is more than that. Our research shows that, as meetings become more time effective, they yield better results and stimulate valuable participation by team members. Applying the above suggestions, the manager is in a better position to make final decisions. Henry David Thoreau once said, "It is not enough to be busy—so are the ants—the question is what we are busy about."

At a convenient time after a meeting, review what you wanted to accomplish and what you actually got done in terms of both the content and the process. Review the before, during, and after planning suggested below. Meeting improvement is an ongoing process. Make plans to do better next time.

Managerial Meetings—A Summary

Successful managers

- ✓ meet regularly with their team of immediate subordinates.
- ✓ seek input from their subordinates during these meetings.
- ✓ make decisions using information obtained at meetings.
- ✓ are not seeking consensus, but making decisions that subordinates agree they can implement.
- ✓ prepare the meeting agenda, keep meeting focused, and ensure follow-up tasks are assigned and completed.

Action Planning

Now it is time to do some action planning for improved performance regarding managerial meetings. Given what you now know, write out some of the things that you plan to do regarding meetings over the next few months. Here are some examples:

Before my next meeting with my direct subordinates, I will

- decide who should attend.
- send out an agenda ahead of time.
- state what type of meeting it is.
- show starting and finishing times.

During my next meeting with my direct subordinates, I will

- use a flip chart or white board for clarity.

- get everyone involved.
- start on time and stay on time.
- discourage use of cell phones, e-mail, etc.

After my next meeting with my direct subordinates, I will

- send out a summary of what was accomplished, and what was not.
- ask for feedback as to what can be done to improve our meetings.
- if possible, set up date, time, type, purpose, and agenda for the next meeting.
- ask for possible items to be included in the next meeting.

_____

_____

_____

_____

_____

_____

It is worth remembering that

"waste your time . . . waste your life"—"master your time . . . master your life"

The bad news is that time flies. The good news is that you're the pilot.

Path 3

CONTEXT SETTING

The Bigger Picture

Managers are accountable for setting context for all their subordinates on a regular basis. It is important that subordinates see how their work fits into the larger picture—their boss's job and the organization as a whole. It is also important that they see how their work fits with the work of their peers and colleagues.

Rate yourself below as to how you feel you are setting context with your subordinates:

Self Assessment

Context Setting

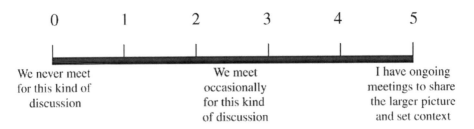

Managers need to share background information on an ongoing basis so that subordinates can make informed decisions and collaborate with their peers and colleagues without having to go back to the manager. Setting clear context for subordinates improves their ability to accomplish their task assignments in relation to the rest of the unit's work. It saves time for the manager and for the subordinates.

There are three types of information sharing. Subordinates need to

- know about the manager's goals and issues so that they can see how their individual work output fits into the unit's work output.
- be provided with the "larger picture" so they understand relevant issues being dealt with by the organization as a whole.
- know about each other's task assignments enabling them to work knowledgeably together and reduce the "silo effect."

Following is an example of a context setting meeting where Jim, the unit manager, is setting context for subordinates on all three types of information sharing:

"As you will recall from my memo, I've put aside time in this meeting to talk about our unit goals and my issues and concerns in reaching them. I have

found that it really helps when we all see what we are striving for as a unit and how each of you contributes to the total output. In this regard, I have been told this morning that we continue to be over budget on the new high-speed copier production line. My boss reminded me that this new line is supposed to contribute significantly to the corporate profit numbers for next year, so we'll have to get our costs down. Hank, what's going on in inventory control?"

"Well, Jim, we've been concentrating on getting the material inventory down for the new high-speed copier production line and that seems to be working. Right now, it's about half of what it was when the line was first launched. This is good for us as we don't have that large supply of parts on our books especially since George tells me there may be some part modifications coming up. And, of course, it gives us more space. We've also developed relationships with some good backup suppliers in the event one or more of our primary ones have trouble delivering on time or their quality drops below our specifications. I'm not sure how much further inventory reduction we should make at this time as production of this copier has been very erratic. Last month, it was shut down for a while. Now I understand there's talk of a second shift because of a surge in demand."

"Thanks, Hank. It looks like you'll have to stay in constant touch with George until this gets worked out. As you point out, keeping the material inventory as low as possible saves a significant amount of money for the company. Now, let's hear from George."

"I'd like to keep discussing the new copier line if I may, Jim. The other assembly lines are mature and running well. Hank and I have been talking about getting the inventory levels down on the mature lines. This should be no problem as the demand is steady and predictable. For some reason, orders for this new copier coming from Sales are all over the place. At times, we can't keep up, and at other times, there is nothing. We do some stockpiling of subassemblies and finished machines. However, with requests for customizing and our continuous modifications, too much stockpiling is a losing proposition. When large orders come in and delivery time is short, we may have to go to a second shift. This needs to be compared to using overtime for the employees on the regular line. Of course, the union is insisting on hiring more workers for a second shift instead of overtime, but this may not be justifiable economically. Right now, we're doing a little of this and a little of that to keep the deliveries

out the door on time. I've talked with Chris, the master scheduler, and he has no idea how to smooth out the demand at this time."

"Okay, George. Let's hope that the demand will soon even out, and as the line matures, we can make an intelligent decision as to go with a second shift or not. Let's you and I meet next week with Chris and see if we can improve the situation."

"Tom, our contracts with the three trucking companies will be up for renewal in two months, and I'd like your input into what changes should be made in the contracts.

"Jim, listening to Hank and George tells me why our shipping has become so unpredictable. Incidentally, our contracts with the three trucking lines we use do not include any clauses for special shipments, such as overnight delivery, and they have been charging us high premiums for this. It makes sense from their point of view as they have to locate an extra vehicle and driver on short notice. If this keeps up, we may want to have our own delivery system for these special circumstances. But this gets us back in the trucking business which we dropped a few years ago."

"You're right, Tom. George may have some ideas before we talk to the trucking firms. Check with him in two weeks to see where all this stands. Then you and I should meet about the contracts."

"You may have heard that next Thursday there will be a Board of Directors meeting here. There has been a request for them to visit the copier machines assembly floor and the ATM assembly area in the afternoon. So if you see some people all dressed up walking around your areas, just smile and answer any questions they may have. Make sure you have extra safety glasses handy."

Context meetings of this type inform each subordinate of issues and concerns of the manager, upper management, and the other subordinates. On occasion, the manager's boss attends the meeting which is beneficial in two ways: he or she describes some of the major issues confronting the department, function, or business unit and learns about the problems and challenges facing management at the lower levels. Context setting can be carried out as part of regular managerial meetings or a special meeting for this purpose.

There are times when context setting is appropriate between the manager and only one of the subordinates. Here, the manager provides context for the subordinate by showing how the completion of his or her tasks fits with the other work that is being done in the unit and by describing the larger outcome the manager is seeking for the total unit.

Setting Context—A Summary

Successful managers

- ✓ set context for their employees on a regular basis.
- ✓ provide the larger picture within which they are working.
- ✓ let subordinates know about issues and concerns of the manager.
- ✓ enable subordinates to know about each other's work.
- ✓ reduce the "silo effect" within the unit and between units.

Action Planning

List some action plans you would like to implement: Here are some examples:

- As a start, schedule a meeting specifically for context setting, inviting your boss to attend.
- Lay out the guidelines and agenda for this meeting in advance.
- Once initiated, set aside part of your regular meetings for context setting.
- Get feedback from the team as to the benefit of this activity and invite suggestions.

_____

_____

_____

_____

_____

_____

Path 4

FEEDBACK

Positive and Constructive

According to many surveys, the most unanswered question in organizations today is "How am I doing?" This can be interpreted as a lack of feedback on the effort individuals invest in their work and the results achieved.

Everyone has an idea as to how they are doing (sometimes a bit self-exaggerated), but feedback from a key person, such as the boss gives the subordinate a unique look at a different reality. It's always important to hear it from the boss. After all, he or she has some control over your progress with the company, including your present and future compensation.

Positive recognition is one of the four factors involved in employee motivation. The other three are achievement, growth and responsibility. Timely positive feedback, when deserved, is a simple way of letting a subordinate know they are important and that they count. It helps build a healthy self-image. It is important to remember that the average worker spends more than 50 percent of their waking hours on the job during their work week.

Does this sound familiar?

"Hi Susan . . . How did your meeting with the boss go?"

"Good, I guess. We agreed on a new time line for next year's budget proposal and an interview date for George's replacement. Not very exciting stuff! However, I took the opportunity to ask him how he thought I have been doing since I've been in the job more than six months now."

"That's very courageous of you! What did he say?"

"I think it caught him by surprise. He didn't say anything for a while, and then said I was doing okay, and that there were a few things I need to learn to become fully functional. I already knew that."

"Did you get the answer you were looking for?"

"Not really. "Doing okay" doesn't do much for me. I would like to hear from the boss some specifics of where I am doing well, in addition to where I need to improve and how to go about it."

"Well, don't expect too much from him on that score. He's not that kind of guy."

Subordinates need to know what they are doing well and where they need to improve. It is the manager's accountability to let subordinates know on a regular basis how they are performing. Depending upon the situation, feedback can be positive, or it can be corrective.

Feedback should be Frequent, Accurate, Specific, and Timely (FAST).

As we have been doing on the other subjects, rate yourself as to how well you believe you are now doing in giving feedback to your direct reports.

Self Assessment

Feedback

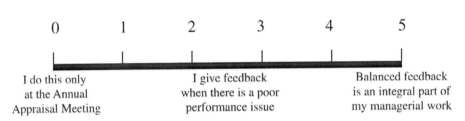

Telling people "you're doing a great job" is not going to have the impact that specific praise, detailed and relevant, could have. Develop a list of "openers" that you can use to keep your praise specific. Here are a few to get you started:

1. "You really made a difference by_____"
2. "I'm impressed with _____"
   "What are the next steps?"
3. "You got my attention with _____"
   "How can we follow up on this?"
4. "You're doing top quality work on _____"
5. "You're right on the mark with _____"
6. "One of the things I enjoy most about you is _____"
   "It's becoming contagious in the unit"
7. "You can be proud of yourself for _____"
8. "We couldn't have done it without your _____"
   "I really appreciate it."
9. "What an effective way to _____"
   "How can we use it elsewhere?"
10. "You've made my day because of _____"

Add a few of your own:

_____

_____

_____

When the opportunity arises, give some positive feedback to a subordinate in a meeting where the person's peers are present. This multiplies the impact many times and will be remembered by everyone. There will also be times when a group, team, or task force should be recognized for extraordinary accomplishment. Select the proper moment for this to happen. Remember the old saying: "Praise in public, criticize in private."

For some managers, giving praise and constructive feedback comes naturally, and they enjoy this aspect of their interpersonal relationships. For most of us, however, we need to develop the feedback habit. This is where feedback reminders come in handy. Here are two real life examples where habits were successfully developed using devices and techniques to support desired behavior.

Feedback Reminders

1. A fish called Feedback

John was in his midforties. As a production engineer, he worked his way up the ladder and became General Manager of the company's largest plant employing more than four thousand people. Things were going very well for him.

One day, John decided that his managers and supervisors (about 200) should get some feedback as to how well they are doing performing their various managerial responsibilities and that this feedback should primarily come from their direct subordinates and subordinates-once-removed. John also participated in the assessment.

The assessment went well, and the responses helped formulate a series of workshops on the subjects needing improvement. One thing happened that surprised John. His own ratings came in high averaging 4.2 on a scale of 0 to 5 (where 5 is the ideal), except for one factor—feedback. When he and I were examining all the data, he didn't want to talk about his feedback score.

A few weeks later, I phoned him on another subject, and the conversation went like this:

"Before we hang up Doctor Fred, I want to tell you what I did about my low feedback score on the assessment. At first, it was hard to swallow as I believe in both positive and constructive feedback, and I think I know how to do it. I came to the conclusion that with everything going on here—the expansion and all—I got into the bad habit of concentrating only on minute to minute and hour to hour things, ignoring one of the ongoing managerial practices critical to the culture at the plant."

"That sounds like the correct diagnosis, John. What do you plan to do about it? As you know, the best way to break a bad habit is with a new habit."

"I've already done it. I bought a goldfish and bowl and put it on my desk. I call the fish Feedback, and it is the first thing I see in the morning when I come to work. Since the fish swims around it is a constant reminder and gets my attention. It may seem a stupid idea, but it works for me. I've improved my old behavior with a new approach. This fish is my reminder."

2. Five Coins

Phil is a CEO who is very good at giving negative feedback. In fact, he enjoys it. However, he would like to be more balanced, but new habits are difficult to acquire without some help.

"Phil, I'd like you to try something that may seem silly at first, but it may work. Take five coins (silver dollars are good), and when you dress in the morning, put all five in your left front pants pocket. They will feel a bit awkward, but this is your reminder. During the working day, every time you give positive feedback, move one of the coins to the right front pants pocket. Try it. It's a simple way to begin a new habit."

About a month later, I called Phil to see how he was coming along.

"Hi Phil, how's your positive feedback habit coming along?"

"I'm glad you called. I tried your somewhat bizarre idea, and for the first week, all the coins ended up where they started in my left pocket. Then I started to move a few, and in two weeks, all five ended up in my right pocket. I stopped using the coins."

"That's great. Do you think you'll keep it up?"

"Absolutely because I see both the reaction in the people and my reaction to their reaction. It has been a real eye-opener for me.

Incidentally, it evens works at home with the family. Thanks again."

Constructive Feedback

There are times when constructive feedback is appropriate. Some people call this negative feedback, corrective feedback, or constructive criticism. It starts early in life from teachers, parents, and older siblings saying such things as "Stop that!", "Don't do that!", and "Do this!" all coming from a parent-child relationship. Over time, as we receive negative feedback, we also learn how to give it. As a manager, we become the parent and the subordinate the child. Constructive feedback works best using an adult-to-adult approach. When giving constructive feedback, focus on what the desired results should have been and not as much on how to do it. Adults learn best not by being told what to do or what not to do something but by experiencing the consequences of their actions. More on this in Path 6, Coaching Subordinates.

Giving Feedback—A Summary

Here are six principles that successful managers follow regarding feedback:

✓ Timely, *positive* feedback is underrated and underused by most managers. Include it in your managerial leadership practices.
✓ Keep your feedback balanced. Many managers tend only to give negative feedback and find it difficult to give praise. Positive and constructive feedback can go together. Remember, when you point a finger at someone, three fingers are pointing back at you.
✓ As with the fish called Feedback, create a device to remind yourself that people want and need feedback about their

performance. This could be a symbol on your mirror, telephone, or computer. It could be an object on your desk.

✓ At a minimum, personal effectiveness feedback should take place every time a subordinate completes a task as given, or lets the manager know she or he may not be able to complete the task to specified QQTR.

✓ Keep the discussion on an adult-to-adult basis, not parent-to-child.

✓ Feedback should be Frequent, Accurate, Specific, and Timely (FAST).

Action Planning

List some possible actions you can take to increase your positive feedback to subordinates and improve your approach to constructive feedback. Here are some examples:

- Create a positive feedback reminder that you see every morning.
- Extend this concept to the evenings and weekends with your family.
- To make positive feedback a habit, keep a temporary log as to your progress in giving positive feedback to your subordinates.
- Plan your constructive feedback prior to the discussion with the subordinate.
- In constructive feedback, focus on the mutually agreed results to be obtained, allowing the subordinate to suggest revisions in procedures.

_____
_____
_____
_____
_____
_____

Path 5

PERFORMANCE APPRAISAL

Informal and Formal

A personal effectiveness appraisal needs to take place every time a subordinate completes a key task or brings a problem of a task assignment for reconsideration. This discussion provides an ongoing appraisal of the subordinate's personal effectiveness. The manager's collection of significant events of this kind is the basis for the manager's periodic informal reviews. At a minimum, each employee should have a midyear and annual review.

The formal annual appraisal meeting acts as a summary of the feedback and coaching meetings that have been held throughout the year. It is part of an ongoing process and should contain few, if any, surprises.

As you have done on previous subjects, rate yourself on how you presently use the annual appraisal meeting:

Self Assessment

Performance Appraisal

Has something like this ever happened to you?

"Hi George, thanks for having lunch with me today. I had my annual appraisal meeting this morning, and it went on for two and a half hours. It was a tough time. I knew it was coming, so I prepared for it. I put together notes on the things the boss helped me through and also some of the things I did very well on my own."

"Did he appreciate your approach?"

"Not really. He asked me what I thought should be my overall rating which I told him, and he responded that it was too high. We then spent the rest of the morning where he defended his rating, and I giving him specific incidents supporting my self-rating."

"How did it end up?"

"I don't know. He said he would need more time to think about it."

Appraising a subordinate should not be a once-a-year exercise, but rather an accumulation of mini-appraisals that happen throughout the year when an assignment has been completed or revised. Most of these will be verbal discussions. Some managers like the idea of keeping a special folder (called a performance folder) for each direct subordinate where notes (good and not-so-good) on the individual's performance are accumulated and referred to at the informal midyear review. Action plans can be established for the second half of the year and the process continues.

By year-end, there then is sufficient data to compile a summary of ongoing mini-appraisals resulting in an overall annual appraisal. Using this method ensures there will be no surprises for the subordinate as significant incidents have been previously discussed and documented. As someone said many years ago, *"The faintest ink is stronger than the fondest memory."*

The manager's collection of significant events of how well a subordinate met the expectations of the key accountabilities of the role is the basis for the manager's periodic reviews and annual summary of personal effectiveness. This information becomes the foundation for the manager's judgment of a subordinate's overall effectiveness.

Guidelines for Performance Appraisal

Successful managers

- ❖ understand that this is not a once-a-year exercise. It is an accumulation of mini-appraisals that occur throughout the year.
- ❖ keep a performance folder on each direct report and put in it any notes, comments, and discussions that have occurred with the subordinate throughout the year. This should include both positive and negative issues. This gives the annual appraisal meeting a foundation of specific incidents and helps to focus on objective data instead of personal opinions.
- ❖ give subordinates ample notice *before* the annual appraisal meeting date and encourage them to prepare for the meeting.
- ❖ allow the subordinate sufficient time to express their view on their effectiveness during the meeting. Listen actively to what they have to say, and let them know you understand their concerns.
- ❖ separate salary issues from the performance appraisal meeting. The meeting should be on the individual's past performance

and potential future growth in the role. Discussing salary issues at this time changes the focus to one of monetary concerns and away from performance.

❖ plan and do a midyear appraisal. This will help bring the subordinate up-to-date on any performance issues that need improvement and any task assignments that need revision. Waiting for a once-a-year annual appraisal is less effective and not recommended.

❖ plan how the formal meeting will happen. Focus on two things: the accomplishment of the tasks assigned to the role and the development of the individual in the role. Many times the annual appraisal is looked at only as a function of salary considerations

❖ have the formal meeting in a neutral setting, not across the desk in a manager-subordinate positioning. Stop all phone calls or other interruptions. Give the subordinate the opportunity to feel equal in terms of communicating facts, opinions, and feelings.

❖ Keep in mind that there are subtle distortions that could distract from a proper appraisal, such as:

  o A tendency to judge overall effectiveness based on the subordinate's most recent behavior.
  o Judging all subordinates at or near average.
  o Giving only above average ratings to avoid confrontation.

Action Planning

List some actions you can take to improve the informal and formal performance appraisal of your subordinates. Here are some examples:

• Create a performance folder for each direct subordinate and add written notes and comments, both positive and negative, throughout the year.
• Do a midyear appraisal which will give the subordinate insight as to your judgment of his or her performance to date and

help the subordinate set plans for the remainder of the
year.
- Give the subordinate ample time to prepare for the formal
annual appraisal.
- During the discussion, allow the subordinate sufficient time
to express his or her viewpoints and actively listen to them.

_____

_____

_____

_____

_____

_____

Path 6

COACHING SUBORDINATES

Growth within the Role

Skilled coaching is one of the critical paths to effective Managerial Leadership. It is not to be confused with training, mentoring, counseling, or teaching (see Definition of Terms section). Each has its place, but the focus of managerial coaching is

- to help the subordinate acquire any additional needed skills in the role.
- to identify areas needing improvement for performing effectively in the role.
- to help the subordinate understand the full range of her or his role.

Managerial Coaching is an interactive process between the manager and the subordinate directed toward the performance improvement of the subordinate in his or her role.

When a manager takes on the role of coach, he or she needs to keep four things in mind:

1. The manager is in a power position which can affect the dynamics of the situation.
2. The issue in question should be specific, not general in nature.
3. The manager has responsibilities to the organization in relation to the subordinate's performance.
4. The manager should believe that the subordinate values the work in the role and wants to improve.

Managers are accountable to be proactive coaches, helping subordinates to understand the full range of their roles and what they need to do to perform the work of that role effectively.

Managers coach subordinates using adult learning principles. Adults learn not by being told but by experiencing the consequences of their actions.

Rate yourself as to how you feel you are doing as a coach to your subordinates:

Self Assessment

Coaching

| 0 | 1 | 2 | 3 | 4 | 5 |

When something is not going right, I explain to them what is wrong and tell them to fix it

I coach by telling subordinates the right way to do something

I coach my subordinates to achieve the desired results from their role

"Good morning, George. I'm looking forward to your report so I can discuss it at the senior management meeting this afternoon."

"Well, I'm sorry, boss, but it won't be ready until next week—something beyond my control."

"Why? What happened? This isn't good."

"Well, everything was working fine. The data was coming in on time, and I left a week for Anna to pull it all together. But Anna came down with the flu, and she's not due back until next week."

"My manager won't be happy. George, what could we have done to prevent this problem from happening?"

"Well, I made what I thought was a sound assumption that Anna would have ample time to pull all this together. It never entered my mind that she wouldn't be available."

"George, let me ask you again. You had an important task assignment with a specific completion date. What went wrong?"

"I made an assumption that turned out to be wrong."

"What can you do in the future to not have this happen again?"

"This has never happened to me before. I learned an important lesson—always have a contingency plan, a plan B, when you make a key assumption. For example, I could have had Shirley shadow this project enough for her to take over in an emergency. It would also give her a development opportunity which she would like. I can assure you this will never happen again."

"George, it is good that you learned something from this incident. However, you still dropped the ball by not letting me know in time for you and me to do something about it right away. Is that a fair conclusion?"

"Yes, I guess so. I didn't realize how important this was. And I made a mistake not keeping you informed of the situation as soon as I realized there was a potential problem. That's the second lesson I learned. It won't happen again."

The above is a real-time incident where the manager coached the subordinate into an improved behavior. Note that the manager was not telling the subordinate what to do differently but allowing the person to state what went wrong and describe acceptable future behavior.

This is an example where the problem was clear, and the subordinate motivated to do better next time. Many times, managerial coaching can be accomplished through a simple process of allowing the person to analyze what went wrong and plan future improvement, such as what was done here. However, there are times when the issues are larger in scope and will take more time and effort to resolve.

The following process can be used as a guideline for most managerial coaching situations:

A Five-step Process for Managerial Coaching

Step One: State Purpose of Meeting

When meeting with the subordinate, be clear what the purpose of the discussion will be. Describe the situation as you have observed it. Use specific incidents and facts to support your case. Define the desired outcomes and the expectations you would like to see as a result of this discussion.

Step Two: Listen to Subordinate

Give the subordinate the opportunity to respond. Try to get agreement on the facts. Listen carefully.

When the subordinate is finished explaining the situation from his or her viewpoint, use open-ended questions to approach mutual understanding of the issue. For example, "What do you think is the problem here?" or "What do you see as the results we should be expecting?"

It is important for the manager and subordinate to come to agreement as to what the problem or issue is and that something needs to get done to mutually solve it. Without this agreement, any solution will be marginal at best.

Step Three: Get problem agreement

Before identifying solutions, it is critical that the subordinate understands and agrees with the desired outcomes as covered in Step Two. A collaborative approach can then be used to explore possible actions.

It is very tempting to tell the subordinate what she or he should do. However, before the manager offers his or her solution(s), the subordinate should be asked to suggest ways to handle the situation and achieve the expected performance. Many times, it is the subordinate who is the best resource for insight and problem-solving, especially in developing ideas for overcoming barriers to improved performance. Here again, good use of open-ended questions will move the discussion in the desired direction and give the subordinate joint ownership of the final action plan. For example, "How would you go about solving this problem?" or "What are some ways we can reach our goal?"

As the discussion continues, a number of options for solution will evolve, some from the subordinate and some from the manager.

Step Four: Establish Joint Action Plan

It is now time to put together an agreed upon action plan. To be effective, it is essential for the subordinate to be an active participant in this process. Having the subordinate suggest next steps and a time line is helpful. It is also a good idea for the manager to ask the subordinate how she or he can help in accomplishing the action plan. A review of the final plan should be done by the manager at this time.

Before making the assumption that the problem is resolved, the manager should ask the subordinate to summarize what was accomplished in the meeting, especially the detailed action plan agreed upon (with next steps and a time line). This ensures that the manager and subordinate have the same understanding of what is to happen. Any discrepancies in the understanding of the agreed-upon action plan are handled at this time. Notes should be taken by both people.

Step Five: Follow-Up

The manager then sets one or more follow-up dates to review progress. Supportive feedback during the follow-up meeting in the form of positive comments and suggestions to the subordinate would be appropriate. Praise is a powerful motivator. If sufficient progress is not apparent, the manager will need to review with the subordinate the reasons why and jointly revise the action plan as appropriate.

The following example illustrates the five-step managerial coaching process in action:

"Good Morning, Pat. Please sit down. We need to visit for a few minutes.

I was talking to Bill over in Accounting last Monday. He mentioned that he is not getting the data from us that he needs every Friday, and it causes his people to have to submit a revised report when he does receive the data. As you know, as Manager of Compensation and Benefits, one of your important assignments this year is to meet with the accounting folks and develop a streamlined process to deliver in a timely way what they need and what the new SAP system requires. How is that coming along?"

"I know, George. The completion date on that is the end of this month, but there's no way I can get it done by then. I was meaning to talk to you about this."

"Pat, I was looking over your key accountabilities for the year, and it seems that you are running behind on a number of them. Am I correct?"

"Well, yes. That's right, but I hope to catch up in the next few months. I have been working late most days, but there doesn't seem to be enough time to do everything."

"Pat, you are a very hard and loyal worker, and I'm glad you're on our team. However, I really want to see you get caught up on your key accountabilities. What do you think is the problem?"

"As I see it, George, it is a time problem. On my white board each morning when I arrive, I list the things I need to do to work on my key tasks, the ones that were established at the beginning of the year. I have no problem scoping these out and planning to get them done. However, and as you know, I am the spokesperson for our area on cross-functional issues. Even problems within our function are directed to me to discuss and help resolve. These are usually one-on-one discussions with another person. With the rapid expansion of the organization, more and more of these critical discussions are being scheduled.

I must say that, given my problem-solving talent and interpersonal skills, I enjoy doing this kind of work very much. Sometimes, the discussions go beyond the initial subject, but I like helping people with their problems.

I only schedule these meetings in the morning so I can get other things done in the afternoon. Each meeting takes about one hour, so only three can be scheduled for any given day. Sometimes, I do one over lunch. My present backlog is over two weeks long."

On top of this, I have another project I am working on that takes at least five hours per week. This is the Continual Improvement project that I suggested at our last team meeting and you assigned to me. It is a significant project, and I am happy to be the lead person on it. It will save us a good deal of time and resources when it becomes operational which I would estimate in about six months. When successfully implemented, the concept can be exported to other parts of the organization for additional savings.

It is these two important ongoing activities that are interfering with my staying on top of the other assignments you have given me."

"Pat, you described the situation very well. I certainly hadn't looked at it this way. As you said earlier, it seems to be a time problem. I would suggest it may also be a priority issue. Let's examine what you can do differently without staying late every evening."

"Yes, George, I will need your help in setting priorities. I'd like to start with the problem-solving sessions which are taking up half of my time every day. In the beginning, I could fit the discussions in, but now they have grown in number and duration. Of course, we could train someone else to share this

load, like Betty for example, but this would take more time up front. Everyone that could do this type of work already has a full workload."

"Pat, you said that you really enjoy helping other people with their work problems as they interface with our function. You also said that sometimes the discussions drift away to other subjects that need attention and, if solved, would help the organization as a whole. Is that correct?"

"Yes, that's true. I look forward to helping other people, and they seem to be very appreciative. However, I've got to do something about this as it is definitely interfering with my other key assignments."

"What could you do to reduce the time spent on these discussions in half. . . . ninety minutes instead of three hours? That's thirty minutes per person instead of sixty minutes."

"Well, I could schedule only Tuesdays and Thursdays for these meetings, but that would create a huge backlog. I could schedule only two per morning instead of three but again, that would result in a constant backlog. I wonder if I could accomplish the main thrust of the session in thirty minutes instead of sixty minutes. It would mean staying on target, working from a structured approach, and only confronting the immediate situation without trying to solve all the other side issues. It would also mean keeping a three per day schedule with little or no backlog."

"I like your idea of a more structured format. You may find that this approach will work for you. It certainly is worth a try. If you can develop a one-page form, a template that the individual completes before the meeting which follows a sound decision-making sequence, it will save a good deal of time. It will enable the individual to think about problem definition, barriers, goals, and options before meeting with you. Completion of the form will also give the person insight into how to solve the problem without coming to you to solve it for them. What do you think?"

"I like it, George. I'll start on this right away. The other subject I mentioned was the continual improvement project which I am heading that takes at least five hours of my time each week."

"How is that coming along, Pat?"

"Slowly, but we're making some headway. Paul is doing the heavy lifting right now. He's a great help."

"Pat, it's important that you get caught up on your key assignments. What do you think of the idea of having Paul take over the project for the rest of the year with your involvement being only one of coaching Paul from time to time?"

"Well, I really like managing the project, but it makes sense to put Paul in charge at this time. It will free up valuable time for me. Between that and the change in my cross-functional problem-solving meetings, I should have no problem getting my regular work done. Thanks for your help, boss."

"Great! Let's get together in a month to see how things are going. Tell Irene to put it on my schedule at a time convenient to you."

The above example illustrates where the subordinate, over time, allowed work preferences to interfere with her role accountabilities and needed some coaching before the situation deteriorated further. Also, the manager, in delegating the Continual Improvement project to her, did not factor in the additional time required. For both George and Pat, this coaching meeting was successful.

As stated in the beginning of this chapter, coaching is one of the most critical skills required of managers. It takes time and a commitment to help others in developing within their present role. (This is not to be confused with developing people for future roles. This is best done by the manager's manager.)

The coaching relationship is a collaborative one between the manager and the subordinate. It can be described as "How can *we* solve the problem." It involves jointly identifying the performance problem, agreeing upon goals to achieve improvement, and determining specific action plans with time lines.

Managerial Coaching Guidelines

❖ Initiate the process in a timely manner and when you feel the subordinate is ready to participate.

❖ Select a location for the meeting that will be free of interruptions.

❖ Be descriptive, not evaluative. Describe actual behavior, not your judgments on the behavior. This will help avoid putting the subordinate on the defensive.

❖ Ask open-ended questions where a yes or no reply can't be given.

❖ Listen attentively—you cannot talk and listen at the same time. A good ratio would be 70 percent listening and 30 percent talking.

❖ Paraphrase the subordinate's responses for clarity and mutual understanding.

❖ Keep the focus on the performance problem and solution, not on the overall individual.

❖ At the end of the meeting, ask the subordinate to summarize the discussion, including next steps and time lines.

❖ Take into account both the subordinate's needs and the organization's needs, resulting in a win-win situation.

Action Planning

List below some of the things you can do to improve your managerial coaching effort.

Here are some examples:

• By (date), decide what coaching sessions you should conduct within the next three months.

• Before your next managerial coaching session with a subordinate, review the five-step process above and plan the discussion.

• Prior to a coaching session, prepare your opening statement which will put the subordinate at ease, and at the same time, be clear as to the purpose of the meeting.

• Develop skill in using open-ended questions where a yes or no answer can't be given.

• Practice paraphrasing an individual's remarks so that you will be able to do this easily during a coaching session.

COACHING SUBORDINATES

Path 7

CONTINUAL IMPROVEMENT

Processes, Systems, and Procedures

As with the preceding paths, continual improvement is integrated into the manager's role. Improving the unit's processes, systems, and procedures is an ongoing managerial leadership practice and, like the others, becomes a habit that will lead to a higher level of performance for the entire unit.

In Nancy Lee's book *The Practice of Managerial Leadership* (mentioned in the opening chapter), she lists four steps necessary to have a successful continual improvement effort in an organization:

1. Hold managers accountable for the process.
2. Maintain an ongoing analysis.
3. Review and prioritize improvement projects and assign as a task.
4. Provide assistance from staff specialists.

Improvement in a process, system, or procedure is seldom an accident or a normal progression of events. It is almost always the result of a conscious effort of one or more people to upgrade an activity so that it can be done more efficiently or produce better results. This can mean less time involved, less manpower used, higher quality, or increased quantity and, of course, reduction in costs.

Developing a plan to embed continual improvement into a manager's ongoing activities may not seem as pertinent as the other six paths. The primary reason for this is that, given the manager's busy minute to minute schedule and overall workload, improvement in general has no specific completion date; it can be put off, postponed for a rainy day. "If it isn't broken, don't fix it" can become the operational attitude. However, research has shown that the best time to improve things is while they are still functioning, before they become ineffective.

On the scale below, rate yourself as to how well you feel you are doing on this important managerial leadership practice:

Self Assessment

Continual Improvement

Continual improvement of work processes is the accountability of each manager. Managers prioritize a list of improvement projects and share this list with his or her manager (up) and subordinates (down). It is reviewed on a regular basis. At any one time, there will be at least one improvement project assigned as a task to an individual in the unit or to an ad hoc team.

Two phases are suggested in a continual improvement effort, one ongoing and one specific:

Phase I

Create an environment where subordinates openly offer suggestions for improvement at any time. This allows for spontaneity. The manager maintains a list of these suggestions and adds his or her own.

The manager needs to refrain from saying to a subordinate, "*That's a good idea. Send me a report on this with all the details—why, how, who, time, and cost/benefit analysis.*" This approach to a suggestion seldom goes anywhere as it becomes a burden rather than an opportunity. It will be interpreted as extra work and will inhibit future suggestions.

Phase II

Set aside all or part of a managerial meeting to identify possible improvement projects. It is important for the manager to involve her/his subordinates in the identification and subsequent development of improvement projects. They will have some good ideas, and there will be synergy. In addition, their involvement now will help later in the implementation stage.

Here are seven steps that will help in launching a continual improvement effort:

1. The manager maintains a list of suggested improvement projects.
2. Periodically, usually quarterly, the manager holds a meeting with his or her immediate subordinates to review the list and add new ones that come up during the meeting and delete those no longer relevant. This meeting can be part of a regularly scheduled managerial meeting or a separate meeting held for this purpose.
3. The list is then prioritized with the help of the team. This is not a consensus activity; the manager makes the final decision and reviews the list with her or his manager for concurrence. The manager's manager can help by discussing what other units may be doing on the same subject, thus eliminating duplication of effort.

4. The manager then delegates the top priority project to a subordinate as a task assignment and part of that person's key accountabilities, making sure that adequate resources (time, funds, expert help, etc.) are available to the subordinate. It is not just adding another project to someone's already full workload. Delegating a CI project to a subordinate becomes part of that subordinate's task assignments, and something else that person is presently doing may have to be minimized, postponed, or given to another subordinate. Like all task assignments, the format should follow the formula laid out in Path 1, Managerial Planning and Task Assignment, specifying a "what by when."

5. If the project appears large in terms of scope, time, and other resources, the manager may create an ad hoc task force to work on the project often involving persons from other areas. If desired, the manager can appoint someone to be leader of this temporary project team and report back to the manager on a regular basis.

6. As improvements begin to be implemented, new ones can take their place. There should always be one improvement project underway at all times.

7. On occasion, an improvement project will include the cooperation of another function. Here, the manager needs to work collaboratively with the manager of the other function to achieve an effective outcome. Clarity of the goal and each individual's accountability is critical in this cross-functional endeavor.

The following is an example of a Continual Improvement meeting I recently witnessed:

"It's good that we all have the opportunity to review the list of possible improvement projects. I have one I'd like to add."

"Go ahead, Paul, that's what this meeting is all about."

"Well, it has to do with our selection process, especially the candidate interview and evaluation part. Although the final decision is with management, we in Human Resources handle all of the administration from preparing role

specifications to contacting search organizations, to arranging to bring in candidates for interviews and so on. It's part of our job, and we've been doing it for years. However, the scheduling of candidates to come in and be interviewed by appropriate managers has never worked well. Emergency meetings, unexpected travel, and other kinds of last-minute schedule changes cause a less-than-professional picture of the overall process. Last week, a candidate arrived, and there was only one manager available to interview her, and that manager was a substitute for someone else. The other two managers that were scheduled for interviews became "unavailable." The substitute manager spent thirty minutes with the candidate and his evaluation form was only partially filled out. It looks like we'll be bringing that person back again. All this costs extra money and resources."

"You're right, Paul. And with the proposed expansion next year, it will get worse. Do you think we can improve the process?"

"I am absolutely sure we can. I've been talking to my colleagues in other companies and reading up on some new approaches, and there is much we can do to improve our method."

"Well, Paul, it sounds like we should put this on the list and give it a priority ranking. What do the rest of you think? How long would it take to make some needed changes in our process and what costs might be involved? Frank?"

"I have been talking to Paul about this. I believe some good candidates have turned us down because of the poor impression we make at the interviews. Other than people's time, there is little cost involved. In fact, we can save money by making the process more efficient and, at the same time, more effective. Paul and I think it would take about two months to develop and recommend a revised approach to our selection process."

"Looks like a winner. If we get approval from my boss, we'll need to juggle some assignments around to get this moving. Thanks for that suggestion. Are there any others to add to the list?"

Continual Improvement is more than a managerial practice. It is a way of life. W. Somerset Maugham, the great novelist once said, "It is a funny thing about life. If you refuse to accept anything but the best, you very often get it." The opposite is also true. If you go through life accepting the status quo, you'll end up with the ordinary, the just "getting by."

As a manager and as a leader, continual improvement points the way for you and your team to become extraordinary in a world of the ordinary.

Continual Improvement—A Summary

✓ Improvement doesn't just happen; it must be a conscious effort.
✓ Continual improvement should be part of a manager's accountabilities.
✓ Managers should have a prioritized list of CI projects, reviewing them on a regular basis.
✓ Managers should create an environment where CI suggestions are welcome for consideration.
✓ Periodic meetings on CI *with subordinates* bring up new ideas and allow participation in the implementation of key projects.
✓ Some key CI projects may involve many people from within and outside the unit. An ad hoc task force may be needed.
✓ There should always be at least one CI project underway at all times.

Action Planning

Write down a few things you could do to begin or improve your efforts in this area. Here are some examples:

• At your next management meeting, bring up the subject and ask your direct reports to think about some projects that would be beneficial to implement. Tell them that we will set aside some serious time at the next meeting for discussion and prioritizing a list of key CI projects.
• Have your list ready for this meeting. Discuss each one and ask for suggestions. Use a flip chart or white board to make revisions and add new possible projects.

- Start with one key project that everyone is enthusiastic about.

_____

_____

_____

_____

_____

_____

7 Paths to Success

In my consulting experience, there are four critical factors that differentiate the average manager from the outstanding one. They are the foundation of effective management and are covered in this book through the practices described in the 7 Paths. The four factors and their relevant practices are:

1. **Achieving Results**
    Path 1: Managerial Planning and Task Assignment
    Path 2: Managerial Meetings
    Path 3: Context Setting

2. **Developing Subordinates**
    Path 4: Feedback
    Path 5: Performance Appraisal
    Path 6: Coaching Subordinates

3. **Influencing the Business**
    Path 1: Task Assignment and Linkage to Strategy
    Path 7: Continual Improvement

4. **Personal Growth and Effectiveness**
    The eight self-assessments and action planning
    The Practices Calendar

You are now familiar with the 7 Paths. As a manager, you are probably doing some of the activities that have been covered but not in the depth and detail that the paths are described in this book. At this point in your reading, you can make a decision as to next steps you may wish to take. Here are some options to consider:

You can put this book on the shelf and say to yourself *"Well, I learned a few things, and when I have some time, I'll start following one or more of the paths."* As we all know, this approach seldom works. The time will never be just right. The thought is well-meant but wishing is not a strategy. Hope is not a plan.

However, if you feel you are not in your "managerial comfort zone" and that the 7 Paths make sense and fit with where you want to be, then don't wait. Use one of the following two options:

1. Review your self-assessments on the practices contained in the 7 Paths. Locate them on the Quick Reference Guide on page 83. Start where it is the easiest. For example, you may choose to work on improving something you already have underway, to restructure your next management meeting, or to review all subordinates' task assignments and convert them to the QQTR format. Start wherever it makes the most sense. But do start.
2. Start where you feel you have the most to gain, where the gap between your self-assessment and the ideal is the greatest. This will give you the highest return on your investment of time and energy.

Practicing the 7 Paths to Managerial Leadership enables the manager to replace poor habits with new good ones. That is a very effective way to change behavior. *Thinking* about and *developing* these new habits will ultimately result in a new and exciting future for you as a manager of others. There is an old proverb that says:

"Our thoughts become our words
Our words become our actions
Our actions become our habits
Our habits become our character
Our character becomes our destiny"

As Peter Drucker, the management guru once said, *"Managerial leaders are not made, they are grown."* Going down the 7 Paths is an excellent way for a manager to develop into an outstanding managerial leader. Managerial Leadership is defined by accomplishing goals, not by possessing certain attributes, by actions not position power. The 7 Paths will orient your thinking and actions for doing just that.

Best wishes in growing into an outstanding managerial leader!

Using the Practices Calendar

As you become familiar with the 7 Paths to Managerial Leadership, you will need a plan to get started and maintain momentum. This is where the managerial leadership practices calendar comes in handy.

Following is an example of a completed calendar. As you can see, it is laid out with the twelve months of the year across the top and the 7 Paths down the side. Various letters allow planning by month and by practice. In this example, the manager

- scheduled three context setting meetings during the year (in conjunction with three managerial meetings).
- scheduled two performance appraisal meetings with each subordinate (informal midyear and formal at year-end).
- scheduled a number of individual coaching sessions with different subordinates.
- included monthly reminders to give feedback to subordinates.
- scheduled periodic meetings with each subordinate on the status of their key task assignments.
- scheduled managerial meetings on problem-solving and other issues.
- scheduled periodic meetings to assess the key continual improvement projects.

As items are accomplished, they can be crossed off in red which offers a visual image of progress being made.

The completed calendar gives the manager an overall look at the current year, what has been accomplished and what has not been done in terms of the managerial leadership practices.

Managerial Leadership Practices Calendar

Year_____

Path	Jan	Feb	Mar	Apr	May	Jun	Jul	Aug	Sep	Oct	Nov	Dec
Task Assignment	T			T			T			T		
Managerial Meetings	M		M		M			M		M		
Context Setting	X				X					X		
Feedback	F	F	F	F	F	F	F	F	F	F	F	F
Appraisal						A						A
Coaching	C						C			C		
Continual Improvement			I			I			I		I	

X = Context Setting Meeting   A = Performance Appraisals

C = Coaching Session   F = Feedback Reminders

T = Task Assignment Status   M = Managerial Meetings

I = Continäl Improvement Review

Quick Reference Guide

Ideas and Guidelines

Definition of Terms

Accountabilities (Key)

These are the most important task assignments and general responsibilities given to an employee that account for about 80% of the person's output.

Appraisal

Periodic discussions of the manager's judgment of a subordinate's effectiveness; the annual appraisal summarizes these discussions.

Authority

The power vested in a person by virtue of his or her role to expend resources: financial, material, technical, and human.

Calendar of Practices

A 12-month planning map indicating actions to be taken on the 7 Paths to Managerial Leadership.

Closure Verbs

Verbs that describe completion when writing a task assignment.

Coaching Subordinates

Assisting a subordinate to (a) handle a task in her or his role more effectively and (b) to understand the full scope of the role and be able to fill it more completely.

Context Setting

Regular updating of the "bigger picture" within which a subordinate's work is carried out.

Counseling

Directed toward behavioral problems (alcohol, drugs, etc.) effecting work output, normally done by outside specialists.

Courage

The ability for the manager and the subordinate, each to speak frankly to each other (adult to adult) on important issues without fear of negative consequences.

Decision

The making of a choice with the commitment of resources.

Delegation

The act of assigning a task to a subordinate.

Feedback Reminders

Developing a habit of utilizing the feedback process with subordinates through the use of symbols, methods, and techniques.

Feedback (Positive and Constructive)

Praising a subordinate when something good was accomplished (positive) and telling a subordinate when results are not up to expectations (constructive).

Filter (Human Forces)

The many factors that distort an employee's work behavior away from what is theoretically expected.

General Responsibilities

That portion of a subordinate's accountabilities that are ongoing in nature.

Improvement (Continual)

Part of the manager's accountability to seek out and implement improvement projects within his or her control. This can be a process, a system, a procedure, etc.

Linkage Process

Through a series of steps, the process of aligning individual key accountabilities and work output to the long-term strategy and goals of the organization.

Manager

A person in a role in which he or she is held accountable not only for his or her own personal effectiveness but also for the work of subordinates.

Managerial Leadership

Combines the discipline of managing a unit with the skill of enabling subordinates to work at their level of capability.

Managerial Leadership Practices

The 7 Paths covered in this book.

Managerial Meetings

Regular meetings with immediate subordinates involving two-way information sharing on a variety of subjects.

Managerial Planning

The manager's determination of task assignments.

Mentoring

The helping of an employee in formulating his or her future plans beyond the present role by someone higher in the organization.

Organizational Structure

A system of roles and role relationships that people are given when they work together. These role relationships establish the boundaries within which people relate to each other.

Output

A product or service produced in a given period of time—a completion of an assigned task.

Project Team

An ad hoc group of individuals brought together under a team leader to complete a specific assignment.

QQTR

When formulating task assignments, Quality, Quantity, completion Time, and Resources available should be described and understood.

Role

Another name for a position or job.

Role Specification

Different from the traditional job description, this document spells out the specific key accountabilities of the role, both tasks and general responsibilities, not just the activities and qualifications.

Self-Assessments

An opportunity for the reader to judge their present proficiencies on the various Managerial Leadership Practices covered in this book.

Seven Paths

The seven critical paths leading to superior managerial leadership.

Silo effect

When work of one group is isolated from another, and communication is essentially vertical and not horizontal; also known as stovepiping.

Skill

An ability (learned through training, practice, and experience) to carry out a given procedure without having to think through the steps involved—sometimes labeled, "unconscious competence."

Task Assignments

Assigning a task to produce a specified output and describing it using QQTR (see above).

Teaching

A general term describing the activity of transferring knowledge or skill to someone else.

Training

The process of improving performance in one or more aspects of an employee's work output through additional knowledge and or skill.

Unit

Any group of people working together toward a common goal with an accountable manager. It could be a section, department, function, etc.

Work

The exercise of judgment and discretion in making decisions in carrying out goal-oriented activities.

Work Planning

The planning by the manager of the work that has to be done, by whom, by when, and how best to use available resources.

Appendix A

ESTABLISHING KEY ACCOUNTABILITIES

Nancy Lee and Fred Mackenzie

Introduction

Key Accountabilities are the most important assignments a manager gives to each subordinate in order to achieve the unit's goals. Clearly describing each employee's key Accountabilities (KAs) is the crucial step in linking corporate strategy to real-time work output. Key Accountabilities are actions for which an employee is held accountable. When delegated properly, KAs offer a clear description of what achievements the individual is expected to accomplish within a specific time frame.

Basic Principles

- Assigning Key Accountabilities and discussing them with each subordinate is not a once-a-year exercise. It is a *continuing process* through which ongoing progress can be gauged of employees' effectiveness in their role.
- Key Accountabilities include both specific tasks with time restraints and general responsibilities that are ongoing in nature with no specific closure. Together, they define the most important assignments—not all of them. They are the ones to be focused on during the time period involved. Tasks are an output the manager needs to have completed by a specific time in the future. General Rsponsibilities are outputs that are needed but are ongoing in nature.
- There is a distinct difference between position descriptions and key accountabilities. As the name implies, position descriptions cover the activities encompassed in the entire role on an ongoing basis. They are useful in the employment process, developmental planning, and determining role level.

Key accountabilities are created by the manager, are time specific, and are directed to a specific subordinate. They are used as part of the performance appraisal, compensation considerations, and the coaching process. Attachment A describes in detail the differences between the two documents.

- Managers decide what tasks they will give subordinates to do. The manager's manager is not to bypass the manager and give assignments since subordinates are each manager's resources to get the work of the unit done.

Assigning Key Accountabilities

Thinking through the most important work that has to be done in a role and discussing it with a subordinate is fundamental to managing. It is this process that helps all employees understand what they are to do. These discussions provide the basis of clarity for subordinates. Committing the results of these discussions onto a document further defines for both manager and subordinate what is expected to happen within a given time frame.

Not all assignments are key, and some need not be listed. In preparing an accountability document for the person in a role, about four to six assignments are typically identified. These are the most important work to be done within the role in the short-term. To achieve full clarity in first-line roles and first-line supervisory roles, it may be necessary to include a few additional KAs.

Key tasks should cover the major thrust of the role for a designated period of time. Typically, 70 percent to 80 percent of all work would be covered. The priority and list of key accountabilities changes from year to year and during the year, as well depending upon overall unit and corporate targets.

Having a clear definition of key accountabilities helps an employee decide where his or her time should be spent each day. For this reason, it is also helpful for the manager to list KAs in order of their importance to the unit.

Preparing Key Accountabilities

Key accountabilities should be planned and established by the person's immediate manager. They are then discussed with the subordinate for agreement as to the achievability of the assignments and any needed revisions are made. These key accountabilities are then reviewed by the manager with his or her manager. The essence of the manager–subordinate relationship is the clear specification of the KAs to be carried out.

The list should be developed and assigned by the immediate manager to each subordinate role; this is by far the preferable method. However, sometimes the subordinate is asked to develop the key accountabilities in *draft* form for editing and approval by the manager. Although it is not recommended, given the time pressure everyone is under, this latter procedure can be made to work *providing* the manager does the important tasks of

(1) having an initial discussion with the subordinate on the content,
(2) reviewing the draft and changing the list to be compatible with other subordinates' KAs and, most importantly, with the manager's own key accountabilities, and
(3) reviewing the document with the manager-once-removed for overall consistency.

The final key accountability document should reflect assignments that are challenging, measurable where possible, attainable, and in line with the manager's accountabilities and the corporate goals.

Having the employee actively participate in the process has important motivational and commitment factors and for clarity of understanding. Employees should feel comfortable asking for clarification on any aspects of the assignment that they do not fully understand.

Assigning Tasks

Managers plan the work of their unit and decide what tasks they will give subordinates to do. They may delegate a task completely to a subordinate or may assign a subordinate to assist in one of the manager's own tasks.

Managers decide on and communicate a task (often calling it a goal or project) having in mind an output that is expected to be generated when the task is completed, e.g. a report to be written, a research project to be completed, calls on customers to be made, a sale to be closed, a rating to be achieved, a percentage to be reduced, and a meeting to be conducted. Output can be a finite product or a service rendered. Output, whether a product or service, is both visible and observable.

When writing a task assignment, the text should begin with a verb that denotes *closure, not* one that describes an *activity*. Some closure verbs are achieve, complete, conduct, identify, obtain, sell. Attachment B is a list of sample closure verbs. Activity verbs, e.g. investigate, analyze, support, assist, monitor are not suitable for defining a task. They can, however, be used in describing a general responsibility which will be discussed later.

In simple terms, a task assignment has three parts: the verb, the subject with metrics when possible, and the timing. Attachment C illustrates the format and gives examples.

QQTR

Key tasks should follow the QQTR format. A task can be defined as a quantity (Q) of things within given quality (Q) limits to be produced by a target completion time (T) within specified resource limits (R).

The manager and subordinate can discuss these parameters to agree on an outcome that is satisfactory to the manager and that the employee believes can be accomplished as assigned. This is an important part of the two-way manager–subordinate working relationship.

Quantity (Q)

There is usually a quantity involved in an output, hence the quantity needs to be specified or understood in the assignment of the task. It may be a number, a percentage, or an item, such as a report, proposal, or plan.

Examples of task quantity include: reduce air travel by 10 percent in 20xx, increase use of online education programs by 20 percent in 20xx, conduct y FCS safety drills by 7/1/xx.

Quality (Q)

The manager specifying output has a quality in mind. There are always quality standards to be met. Too low a quality and the output is unsatisfactory; too high and more resources are used than necessary. The output needs to be provided within certain quality standards, and these standards must be set clearly enough that everyone knows what they are. If a subordinate is to produce a given quantity to that quality, it is necessary to ensure that the quality needed is understood.

Time (T)

A task is not only a "what" but is also a "what-by-when"—that which is to be completed by a targeted completion time. This should be made explicit when assigning a task. The manager plans this target completion time to fit with the other tasks that the manager needs to get done toward achieving the unit goals.

One of the reasons for making the time explicit when assigning a task is that the subordinate can discuss with the manager any problems anticipated in meeting the timing given the resources, quantity, and quality specified. If no target completion time is defined, it is difficult to evaluate task accomplishment.

Tasks can be of any length—a day, a month, six months, a year, fifteen months, eighteen months, two years, etc. Too often managers focus only on what has to be done each year since appraisals are frequently required to be done annually. It is more effective to think of when the most important tasks need to be completed and then to discuss the results with the subordinate at the time of completion. Tasks of longer than a year in duration can have milestone discussions that help the manager evaluate how things are progressing. The annual appraisal then consists of a review of these completion and milestone discussions and contains no surprises.

Resources (R)

Tasks need to be assigned in terms of resources that are available, e.g. the amount of money that can be spent, how many man-hours can be used, what equipment and materials are available. The resources that are available are often not explicitly discussed, but the manager must ensure that the employee understands what they are since R*esources* (R) directly affect the other three parameters (*Quantity, Quality, and Time*). The employee should be clear about what resources are available and if there are concerns to negotiate available resources with the manager.

An example of QQTR is a report that needs to be written. The manager sets context by describing to the subordinate why the report is needed, the topic of the report, an overview of the literature search that needs to be carried out resulting in a survey of at least 80 percent of all identifying writing on the subject published in the last two years. This provides both the *Quantity* and *Quality* expected and a way to consider how effective the employee was in completing the task.

The manager states that the researcher has three months to complete the report (*Time*). The manager tells the subordinate, for example, that there is a budget of $1,500 to cover research expenses and that an intern will be provided to help compile the bibliography (*Resources*). The manager expects the subordinate to work on this report, along with other ongoing work in such a way that the report will be completed on time, as well as all of the subordinate's other assigned tasks.

Policies and Procedures

Although quality standards, policy, and procedure limits are not always explicitly stated, they always exist and are implicitly assumed by both manager and the subordinate. It is a manager's responsibility to familiarize subordinates with these and see that they are adhered to in working on tasks. This is critically important with policies that involve safety or legal liability.

Prioritization and Changing Circumstances

The manager sets priorities for the work of subordinates. Where possible, it is useful to list key tasks in order of priority, adding additional clarity to the document. When a subordinate is not able to complete a task as defined, he/she should go to the manager in time for adjustments to be made. This is often caused by a change in circumstances or prevailing conditions. When this occurs, the subordinate goes to the manager to discuss the situation and, when possible, makes suggestions as to changes that might be made. It is the manager who then makes the decisions and reprioritizes, often adjusting the QQTR of that or other tasks. The goal is to have all tasks completed to QQTR with no unpleasant surprises for the manager.

If there is need for speed

There is an important point that needs to be understood. Both managers and subordinates generally have a good idea of what is a reasonable time needed to complete an assignment. If the manager assigns a task that is to be completed in three months, it is a different task then if the subordinate is given one month to do it. Some people have difficulty with this point and think that it cannot be a different task just because the time allowed is two months less—but it is a different task. The subordinate will have to make different decisions and behave differently. The manager may have to adjust some of the other parameters, such as quality or quantity and perhaps assign more resources, or revise other tasks the subordinate is doing.

With only one month to do the report, the subordinate may decide to do much less research, and the literature review may have to be much more cursory. The employee will have to decide to adjust the work he or she has to do on other tasks in quite a different way because of the allotted time he or she has been given to complete the report.

Depending upon how much time the employee has to spend on the report, he/she will have to consider what can be set aside for now and what cannot, while still completing all of the assignments on time. Where these decisions impact other key assignments the employee will need to discuss these issues with the manager. It is the manager who is the one to adjust some of those other assignments if the report must be finished in a relatively unrealistic time period.

Here, for example, the employee, who now must complete the report very quickly, may ask the manager for temporary clerical help to be assigned to help with certain aspects of producing the report and ask to have the date on another task postponed for several weeks.

What—Not How

In establishing key tasks, it is neither necessary nor desirable to describe how to accomplish the task. That is for the subordinate to decide and is part of the subordinate's work. As long as they remain within the boundaries set by the organization, allowing employees to get on with their work in their own way is what is empowering, creative, and rewarding for employees. When a manager describes how to do a task in great detail (micromanaging), it may indicate

- the employee may not be of the right level to do the work of the role.
- coaching the employee is required to help growth in the job.
- not knowing how or being hesitant to delegate (fear of failure).

An example of too much "how": "By working with the business units discussing their concerns and reviewing the last five years of statistical data, create charts on an excel spreadsheet and analyze trends to determine future actions regarding the avoidable and unavoidable turnover situation. After reviewing the results with the business units, revise and submit a report with recommendations by 10/31/xx."

Although the manager and subordinate may wish to discuss some of the methods to be used, the task might be stated more simply: "By 10/31/xx, submit a report on the present status of employee turnover rate, and recommend actions to be taken to reduce future avoidable turnover."

General Responsibilities

As mentioned above, key accountabilities that are *ongoing* are called general responsibilities. General responsibilities are closer to the things typically described in position descriptions. They do not have a specific time by when they must be completed. However, they occasionally have specific tasks that are imbedded in them which have related target dates involved.

General responsibilities are

- typically limited to four or five that are most important (Key).
- directly related to the goals of the unit and the strategy of the organization.
- specific to the role (*not* universal items e.g. control the budget, build the team, support the strategy, develop subordinates, manage the unit, etc.).

Sometimes, it is desirable to include certain generic statements as part of every employee's key accountability document to support legal requirements or place emphasis on a particular concern, such as safety.

Writing General Responsibilities

- General responsibilities should begin with an action verb, such as: monitor, oversee, provide, participate, maintain, assist, support, etc. Examples of a general responsibility statement are as follows: Revise the company organization charts each time there is a change in personnel.

- Remain current with changes in the OSHA regulations regarding _____.
- Serve on the following committees: _____.
- When changes occur, update the policy & procedures manual quarterly except for safety issues which need to be distributed within one week of approval.

Summary

The foundation of the manager-subordinate relationship is the clear specification of the key accountabilities to be carried out. This clarity of the most important assignments, both key tasks and key general responsibilities, given to subordinates is critical to enhancing trust and achieving the overall success of the organization.

Attachment A

Comparisons

	Position Description (describes the role in general)	Key Accountability Document (provides specific assignments from the manager to the person in the role)
Scope	Everything in role	Key assignments for specific time period
Origin	Human Resources	Managers' accountabilities for specified period of time
Strategy	Not Related	Supports and aligned with the Corporate Strategy
Description	Activities	QQTR
Updating	Seldom	Often, sometimes twice a year
Performance	Not Related	Basis of Appraisal
Utilization	Passive	Dynamic
Verbs	Open ended	Closure
Time	Ongoing	Specific and varies with assignment

Note: It is possible for two incumbents with the same role specifications (position description) to have different key accountability documents for the same time period.

Attachment B

Sample Closure Verbs

Key Closure Verbs	Also Usable	Usable With Added Closure Verb
Achieve	Appraise	Advice and . . .
Audit	Approve	Analyze and . . .
Close	Assign	Apply and . . .
Complete	Attend	Arrange and . . .
Conduct	Authorize	Assure and . . .
Consolidate	Classify	Check and
Eliminate	Construct	Consolidate and . . .
Establish	Create	Describe and . . .
Evaluate	Design	Determine and . . .
Generate	Deliver	Develop and . . .
Identify	Distribute	Inspect and . . .
Implement	Execute	Interview and . . .
Initiate	Issue	Perform and . . .
Manage	Open	Prepare and . . .
Obtain	Provide	Review and . . .
Recommend	Select	Revise and . . .
Schedule	Summarize	Transmit and . . .
Sell	Test	Update and . . .
Submit	Train	Verify and . . .

Attachment C

The Anatomy of a Task Assignment

(closure verb) . . . (metrics: %, #, subject) . . . (completion or milestone date)

Examples

execute	newly approved XX plan	by 7/31/xx
Submit	recommendations for XX	by 8/31/xx
Reduce	avoidable turnover by 20% compared to average for the years 20xx-20yy	by 12/31/xx
Increase	20xx customer satisfaction ratings by 15% over 20yy	by 12/31/xx
Implement	two LEAN process reviews and submit results	first by 7/31/xx second by 11/30/xx
Achieve	profit of minimum $200K from P&S projects	by 12/31/xx
Conduct	CPI/Lean training to 50% of total work force	by 11/15/xx
Provide	up-to-date budget information to XXX for use in managing the budget throughout the year	by end of each month

Appendix B

MAKING STRATEGY WORK— THE LINKAGE PROCESS

Nancy Lee and Fred Mackenzie

Introduction

The linkage process is a method of converting an organization's long-term plans into actual work output. It involves a logical and systematic procedure in which employees, at all levels, actively participate.

There are two compelling reasons for implementing this process. The first is organizational, and the second is individual. Organizationally, it establishes a step-by-step way of ensuring that long-range plans, and objectives are translated into desired results. Individually, it creates understanding of how each employee's work output contributes to the overall goals of the organization. This enhances the motivation of each person since output becomes personal goal accomplishment, not just ongoing day-to-day activity.

Aligning individual assignments with organizational objectives is a win-win opportunity. It is both logical and essential that the sum total of the employees' work achieves the overall objectives of the organization. *The better the fit between work output and corporate strategy, the more outstanding the results, where the ordinary becomes the extraordinary.* Agreeing with this conclusion is easy. Implementing it takes effort.

For objectivity and skill in facilitating the linkage process, it is helpful that an external consultant be used, at least for the initial cycle.

Step One

As in life itself, little progress on anticipated results can be made without first having a mission and a plan.

Having a strategic plan is the first step in the linkage process. It typically begins with senior management determining and then communicating the organization's values, vision, mission, and overall strategy.

With the long-range strategy in place, senior management meets to decide four to six key factors to be focused on that will make the difference in whether the organization is successful or not. These are called critical success factors (CSFs). They are subjects, not action phrases.

Typical examples are growth, profitability, technology, human resources, manufacturing, acquisitions/divestitures, access to capital, and product development.

Step Two

Each of the identified CSFs is broken down into long-range corporate objectives, typically with either a three- or five-year horizon. If doing this is the first time, three years may be the most effective to use. There are usually about four objectives for each CSF. Here, numbers, percentages, milestone, dates, and other metrics are included. These are organizational objectives; individual accountabilities are not delineated at this time.

The formulation of these long-range corporate objectives is generally accomplished in a meeting of senior management where the group is divided into subgroups working within the CSF of their expertise. The findings of the subgroups are then shared with the larger group for understanding and modification. This activity should result in 16 to 24 corporate objectives which all of senior management has participated in formulating. The role of the CEO in this process is paramount as he/she will be held accountable for the end results.

An example of a corporate objective is: "complete two acquisitions within three years, one in the USA and one in Europe."

Step Three

From these corporate objectives, short-term goals are developed. These are usually twelve to eighteen months in duration. On average, there are about three to five short-term goals for each of the long-range objectives yielding anywhere from fifty to hundred corporate short-term goals.

To determine these short-term goals, senior management decides who should work on creating them for each of the corporate objectives. Teams are created to address each of the objectives. Each team develops specific goals from the objective (s) assigned to them and submits the draft to a planning facilitator for consolidation into a list of goals by CSF and objective. All goals are assigned to a functional manager who is accountable for achieving the goal. This list is then distributed to all members of senior management for review prior to meeting as a group.

A group meeting is held to discuss, clarify, and modify as necessary the corporate short-term goals. This meeting may include members of the working teams who are not part of senior management. It is important not to have more goals than senior management believes can be accomplished during the designated time frame.

The end result is a *Master Corporate Document* showing corporate short-term goals, how they relate to long-term corporate objectives, and the critical success factors derived from the strategy. A template is available for this document.

An example of a corporate short-term goal is: "Within eighteen months, identify four potential acquisitions, two in the USA and two in Europe."

Senior management has now participated in formulating, developing, and understanding the organization's specific goals for the near term, as well as the long-term objectives. The process has now moved from the strategic (planning) stage to the tactical (operational) stage.

Step Four

The last step in this process is the linkage of short-term corporate objectives and goals to individual accountabilities. The CEO works with his or her immediate subordinates individually to determine their key accountabilities. Many times, a corporate short-term goal (and sometimes a corporate long-term objective) becomes the key accountability for one of the CEO's immediate subordinates who, in turn, delegates all or part of it to their direct subordinates. It then gets broken down into task assignments for directors, managers, etc. as the assignments cascades throughout the organization.

Some education is required at the beginning of step four for proper crafting of the key accountabilities (important task assignments) by the managers at all levels. This would include the use of a customized key accountabilities document setting out a roadmap for each employee's work output for a given time period. A template is available for this document.

An example of a key accountability is: "Within six months, establish an acquisition task force, have members agree on a plan to proceed, and submit this plan to the CEO for approval."

Conclusion

The *foundation* of the linkage process is the clarity of individual accountabilities as they are cascaded throughout the organization. Managers delegate task assignments to specific subordinates based on corporate goals and objectives.

The *secret* of the effectiveness of this process is in the ability of managers to determine appropriate accountabilities, explain these task assignments to their subordinates so that they understand what needs to be done, and then to allow the subordinate latitude to craft the actions necessary to complete them. The participation of the subordinates is not in *determining* their accountabilities but in deciding *how* they will be achieved.

Linking long-range strategy to individual key accountabilities transforms broad strategic plans into focused operational plans where all employees understand and feel part of the overall direction and thrust of the organization, both in the short-term and long-term.

Linking Strategy to Results

Values, Vision, Mission

Long Term Strategy

Critical Success Factors

Corporate Long-Term Objectives

Corporate Short-Term Goals

CPSIA information can be obtained at www.ICGtesting.com
Printed in the USA
LVOW121239010213

318239LV00001B/2/P